Confronting Disabling Barriers: towards making organisations accessible

John Swain, Maureen Gillman and Sally French

VENTURE PRESS

© John Swain, Maureen Gillman and Sally French 1998

All rights reserved. No part of this publication may be reproduced, stored in a retrieval system, or transmitted, in any form or by any means, electronic, mechanical, photocopying, recording or otherwise, without the prior permission of Venture Press

Published by
VENTURE PRESS
16 Kent Street
Birmingham
B5 6RD

British Library Cataloguing-in-Publication Data
A catalogue record for this book is available from the British Library

ISBN 1 86178 0273 (paperback)

Design, layout and production by
Hucksters Advertising & Publishing Consultants,
Riseden, Tidebrook, Wadhurst, East Sussex TN5 6PA

Cover design by:
Western Arts
194 Goswell Road
London
EC1V 7DT

Printed and bound in Great Britain by
Biddles Ltd, Guildford and King's Lynn

Contents

Acknowledgements	ii
Introduction	1
Section one: Confronting disabling barriers	**3**
A SEAwall of institutional discrimination	5
The Framework of Analysis	5
The Cement of Normality and Independence	7
Experiencing disabling barriers	11
Structural Discrimination	11
Environmental Discrimination	13
Attitudinal Discrimination	15
Constructing Institutionalised Discrimination	17
Analysing professional practice: social work	19
The Context	19
Professional Practice and Institutional Discrimination	19
Constructing Institutionalised Discrimination	23
Section two: Six case studies	**27**
A local authority community care team	29
Discussion	34
Skills for People	39
Discussion	42
Herefordshire Lifestyles	45
Discussion	49
Sirdar Road Primary School	53
Discussion	56
Derbyshire Centre for Integrated Living	59
Discussion	61
A GP practice	63
Discussion	66
Section three: Enabling access	**69**
Changing policies	71
Changing minds	75
References	79

Acknowledgements

We are grateful to the many people who helped us to make this book a reality. We should like to thank all the people we interviewed for the openness with which they talked about their work and shared their thoughts and ideas. Their experiences and views contributed in a very major way to this book. In particular we should like to thank the participants in the following organisations: the local community care team; Herefordshire Lifestyles; Sirdar Road Primary School; and the GP practice.

Our thanks are also extended to Laura Middleton for her helpful comments on an earlier draft and her support throughout.

Introduction

The aims of this guide are to provide social workers, education, health, and welfare professionals with a framework for the analysis of the social and physical barriers that disabled people encounter in their relations with organisations. The framework is intended to help practitioners understand institutional disablism and to enable them to generate possibilities for change and good practice. It is recognised that the influence of professionals upon their organisations may be related to their position in the agency hierarchy and the setting itself. The book is designed to be of use to practitioners, their power and influence notwithstanding.

The discussions within the guide are underpinned by the social model of disability which asserts that disability arises from the socially constructed barriers to transport, employment, education, and leisure rather than from the individual's physical or sensory impairment. Whilst some of these barriers are manifested by the lack of physical access to organisations by disabled people, others are at a structural and attitudinal level; built into organisational policy and culture and maintained by the dominant ideology which addresses the needs of non-disabled poeple.

We think it might be helpful to the reader to define some of the terms used in the guide. The term "organisation" refers to a setting where a group of people are employed to carry out tasks, either for monetary reward or on a voluntary basis. An example of an organisation is a social services area team, or a day centre. "Institution" is used to describe models of thought and action that sustain an organisation. "Social work" itself is an example of an institution. Institutional disablism is therefore discrimination that arises from policies and subsequent practices based upon the dominant discourses of thought and action within an organisation or society at large.

Introduction

The guide is in three sections. The first presents a framework for understanding and analysing institutional discrimination (see Figure 1 p6). It is graphically presented as a wall of barriers to access for disabled people. The foundations of the wall are structural barriers on which environmental and attitudinal discrimination is built. The interaction between the various layers is conceived of in terms of ideologies of "normality/abnormality" and "independence/dependence".

Section two is a series of six case studies of organisations. The purpose is to explore and illustrate the framework provided in section one and to suggest possibilities for making organisations more accessible to disabled people. Each case study is based on documentary evidence or interviews conducted by the authors.

The concluding section reviews possibilities for enabling access, looking particularly at the achievements of the Disabled People's Movement.

Section one:

Confronting disabling barriers

A SEAwall of institutional discrimination

THE FRAMEWORK OF ANALYSIS
The following is our definition of institutional discrimination:

> *Unfair or unequal treatment of individuals or groups which is built into institutional organisations, policies, and practices at personal, environmental, and structural levels.*

Disabled people face institutional discrimination in a social and physical world that is geared by, for, and to non-disabled people. The notion of institutional discrimination has played an important role in the development of theories of disability (Barnes, 1991) generating from a social model and developed by disabled people. It is also a notion that links the experiences of disabled people with those of other groups. The commonalties in issues of racism, sexism, homophobia, and disablism can be explored through themes such as prejudicial attitudes and discriminatory language, whilst also highlighting differences in the forms of discrimination faced by different groups (Thompson, 1997).

Essentially, to understand discrimination as being "institutional" is to eschew individualised, or victim blaming, explanations of unjust treatment. This includes psychological models of attitudes that give no account to the historical and social context of prejudice. In such models, non-disabled people's responses, such as fear, are seen as a direct and inevitable personal reaction to people with impairments. To see discrimination as institutional, however, is to recognise that inequalities are woven into the very structure and fabric of British society and organisations. Discrimination is constructed at different levels within social divisions between disabled and non-disabled people and the power relations that maintain the marginalisation of one group by another.

People with impairments are disabled by institutional barriers that prevent their full participative citizenship in society, access to and participation in organisations. **Figure 1** depicts these barriers as the bricks in a wall of institutional discrimination. The wall (rather than more usual concentric circles) graphically illustrates the marginalisation of disabled people. In this model of institutional discrimination, attitudinal barriers are constructed on environmental barriers, which are themselves constructed on structural barriers. No graphics can depict the interlinking and interaction between the three levels, though, as discussed below, ideology plays a key role in the articulation and interreliance between each layer.

The SEAwall of Institutional Discrimination

Attitudinal	Cognitive prejudice: assumption about the (in)abilities, emotional responses, needs of disabled people	Emotional prejudice: fear	Behavioural prejudice: individual practice and praxis	Cemented by ideologies of "normality" and "independence"
Environmental	Disablist language	Institutional policies, organisation, rules and regulations	Professional practices: assessment, care management	Inaccessible physical environments
Structural	Hierarchical power relations and structures: disempowerment of disabled people	The denial of human, social, and welfare rights	Structural inequalities: poverty	

The foundations of the wall are built at the STRUCTURAL level. Institutional discrimination is founded on the social divisions in society and, in particular, hierarchical power relations between groups (for example, disabled and non-disabled people). Inequalities in the distribution of resources, particularly economic, underpin hierarchical power relations, with many disabled people being marginalised from open employment and condemned to poverty. In recent years the concept of citizenship has also been drawn on in understanding structural barriers (Oliver, 1996). Disabled people, as a group, are denied political, social, and human rights that non-disabled people take for granted.

The ENVIRONMENTAL level of barriers is constructed, on these foundations, in the interaction between the individual and the social and physical environment. These, then, are the barriers confronted by disabled people in relation to rules, procedures, patterns of behaviour, shared understandings, timetables, and so on (i.e. social organisation), that are geared to the needs and norms of the non-disabled majority. The barriers are also created by aids that are geared to the needs and norms of non-disabled people (steps, taps, cars, buses, etc.), the needs of disabled people being marginalised to "special" aids. One major focus for many disabled people is in their relationship with service provision and professional practice, which can play an important role in shaping their lives and enforcing dependency.

The third layer, ATTITUDINAL, which is built on the previous two, is constructed in the direct interactions between disabled and non-disabled people, as individuals or in groups. These barriers are manifest in the attitudes and personal prejudices of non-disabled people, their expectations and actions. This includes the beliefs, feelings, and practices of individual professionals. These relate to, but can differ substantially from, the collective professional practice, including training, ideology, and organisational structures, which is conceived at the environmental level in this model. Thus, our analysis acknowledges that, despite the constraints, individual professionals can and do support the struggle of disabled people against institutional discrimination, even though the general practice of their profession contributes to this SEAwall of barriers.

THE CEMENT OF NORMALITY AND INDEPENDENCE

If each brick in this wall of institutional discrimination was separable from all the others, the wall could be dismantled brick by brick. However, as the Disabled People's Movement has recognised, piecemeal approaches are ultimately ineffective in dismantling institutional discrimination, and it needs to be recognised that all these barriers are closely bound and interrelated. Part of the dynamic of this interlinking is through ideology.

Thompson (1997) refers to ideology as the "glue" that

binds together the levels in his model of institutionalised discrimination. In doing so, a dominant ideology operates in a number of ways:

1. legitimising social inequalities, power relations, and structures;
2. establishing "what is 'normal' and therefore, by extension, what is 'abnormal' " (Thompson, 1997, p 25);
3. defining cultural values and desirable goals;
4. being "naturalised, taken for granted and almost all-embracing" (Barnes, 1996, p 48).

There are a number of dimensions to the ideological basis of institutionalised discrimination faced by disabled people.

a) The individual model: in which disability is seen as a problem, and the problem is located in the impaired individual;
b) The medical model: which is a form of the individual model and strengthens the legitimisation of inequality based on biology;
c) Stereotypes of disabled people;
d) Societal values of "normality:abnormality" and "dependency:independency". These values not only define disabled people as "abnormal", but also as needing care, cure, and control to become, if not normal and independent, then as nearly so as possible. Such ambitions are rarely those of disabled people themselves

(Swain and French, 1998).

The development of the concept of the norm or average in European culture can be traced, as Davis (1995) does, to the early nineteenth century and is associated with the introduction and application of statistics in social research. Closely interwoven with this changing ideology of interpersonal judgement were changes in the social construction of disability. Davis writes:

"the very concept of normalcy by which most people (by definition) shape their existence is in fact inexorably linked to the concept of disability, or rather, the concept

of disability is a function of a concept of normalcy. Normalcy and disability are part of the same system"
(1995: 2).

He analyses *"the notion of normalcy that makes the idea of disability (as well as ideas of race, class, and gender) possible"* (p 159). Judgements of disabled people are, in Western society at least, in accordance with normative criteria whereby we decide whether a behaviour or situation is normal or abnormal by comparing it with the behaviour and situation of the majority. Thus a disabled person would be deemed abnormal simply as measured against the non-disabled majority, and a special school regarded as abnormal simply because most schools are mainstream – indeed they are often referred to as "normal" schools.

The dominance of the ideology of normality:abnormality is such that it is difficult to think of areas of contemporary life in which it is not brought to bear. Its importance in understanding the social construction of disability lies not simply with the dominance of this ideology, however, but also its inherent value basis. Social judgements of normality or abnormality have an inherent value judgement of "desirable" or "undesirable", "good" or "bad", which are given credibility and power by association with the claims of statistics to neutrality and objectivity. Thus, normality and abnormality are seen as social facts rather than interpersonal value judgements. As Drake writes:

> *"the concept of 'normality', far from describing some natural or preordained state of affairs, instead represents an acknowledgement of the values which have come to dominate in a particular community at any given time."*
>
> ***(1996: 147)***

The value basis of the ideology of normality is predominantly negative on the side of abnormality. Abnormality may be judged by considering the contribution the person, or group of people, can make to society, that is, perceptions of their physical and social worth. Disabled people are often thought to be incapable of contributing meaningfully to the community by, for example, becoming parents or engaging in paid employment.

The ideology of independence is closely associated with that of normality and provides a similar basis for rationalising and justifying discrimination (French, 1993a and Oliver, 1993). Independence is defined in terms of notions of what people normally do for themselves, and as with the ideology of normality has both a value based dimension (as a "good") and a conformity dimension (as a "should"). The integral nature of the two ideologies is well illustrated, for instance, by the definition of disability in the Disability Discrimination Act 1995. People are defined as disabled by their inability to carry out "normal day-to-day activities", in turn defined as mobility, continence, manual dexterity, and so on. Thus the SEAwall of discrimination is cemented in the discourses of abnormality and dependency.

There are three main lines of critique of the ideology of independence:

1. The need to redefine independence in terms that are meaningful to disabled people themselves to encompass: not living in an institution; not living in poverty, but having control over finance to purchase services; and having control over decision making processes in daily living;
2. The lack of realisation of the dependent nature of daily living for all. Aids that non-disabled people rely on for mobility (shoes, footpaths, and so on) are taken for granted and disassociated from dependency, while aids for disabled people are seen as meeting "special needs". Wendell states: *"The help that non-disabled people receive tends to be taken for granted and not considered help but entitlement... It is only when people need a different kind or amount of help than that given to 'paradigm' citizens that it is considered help at all, and they are considered socially dependent"* (1996: 41). Thus, "social ideals must change in the direction of acknowledging the realities of our interdependence and the value of depending on others and being depended upon" (Wendell, 1996, 151);
3. The third critique argues that dependency does not derive from the functioning of the individual, but is created and enforced by institutional discrimination. Thus, Oliver writes: *"disabled people are likely to face exclusion from the workforce because of their perceived inabilities, and hence dependency is... being created"* (1993: 51).

Experiencing disabling barriers

STRUCTURAL DISCRIMINATION
At a structural level, institutionalised discrimination is built into British society as a whole, and what might be called the macro-systems: economic, education, and welfare. Oliver and Barnes describe the ideas of institutional discrimination in the following ways:

> "First, institutional discrimination is evident when the policies and activities of public or private organisations, social groups and all other organisational forms result in unequal treatment or unequal outcomes between disabled and non-disabled people. Second, institutional discrimination is embedded in the work of welfare institutions when they deny disabled people the right to live autonomously, through failure to meet their statutory obligations in terms of service provision, through their differential treatment of legislative and advisory codes, through interference in the privacy of disabled people and through the provision of inappropriate and segregated services."
>
> *(1993, pp 274-5)*

In this second part of Section one, we turn to the experiences of the SEAwall of institutional discrimination as documented by disabled people. As, throughout a guide of this nature, our discussion is necessarily selective we shall concentrate first on economic disadvantage.

Poverty underlies the marginalisation of disabled people in the UK and for many disabled people is central to the substantially poorer quality of life they experience, compared with the rest of the population. The statistics from a succession of surveys (such as Martin and White, 1988) highlight considerable disadvantage:

> *"Comparisons with the equivalent incomes of the general population showed that families with a disabled member below retirement age had significantly lower incomes than those without a disabled member – 72% lower."*
> *(Barnes, 1991, 99)*

Such bare figures are reinforced by documented personal experiences.

Anita Binns, a woman with learning difficulties, states:

> *"One of my biggest things is money. I live on my own so I get help with my rent and I get help with my Poll Tax, but if they gave me enough money I would be able to pay it. I get so much Severe Disablement Allowance and I get Income Support. It's so little. They give me a rise on one hand and they take it off me in another. In fact at times I find it really difficult to make ends meet. I'm robbing Peter to pay Paul."*
> *(Swain, 1993)*

As this quote begins to indicate, statistics belie the complexities of poverty which are related not only to lower levels of income but also the extra financial costs associated with impairment. Furthermore, overall statistics underestimate the poverty experienced by different groups of disabled people, particularly disabled women and black people.

As French (1998) states:

> *"Disabled people are far more likely to be unemployed than non-disabled people and the situation is particularly bleak for black disabled people and disabled women."*

The statistics in relation to income testify not only to the high levels of unemployment, but also to substantial underemployment. In her paper analysing the employment opportunities for visually disabled people, French (1998) documents statistics from two surveys showing that visually disabled people in employment are far less likely (approximately 70%) to be in professional jobs than non-disabled people.

Explanations of unemployment, underemployment, and poverty can focus on the different levels of discrimination – structural, environmental, and attitudinal. The SEAwall model, like other analyses by disabled people, starts at the structural level. Oliver (1991), for instance, argues that disabled people are, by and large, excluded from labour market participation because of changes in the work process that occurred with the coming of industrialised capitalist society. The crucial importance of the structural level is emphasised, too, by Finkelstein (1993) who argues that levels of employability and participation in the creation of social wealth is "the predominant factor" in the creation of disability.

Reviewing the evidence relating to increased expenditure, Barnes (1991) points to three types:

> *"capital expenditure on lump-sum purchases, regular expenditure on items related specifically to impairment, and expenditure on items required by most people, but on which disabled people need to spend more."*
>
> *(p 99)*

He concludes that, in general, such expenses amounted to 8% of all disabled adults' disposable income.

Environmental Discrimination

The hierarchy of social divisions is built into social institutions and organisations through formal arrangements that govern social interactions between people. These formal arrangements, such as fire regulations, rigid timetables, and assessment and exam regulations can restrict certain groups of people. Discrimination is also encountered by disabled people in their daily interactions with the physical world of non-disabled aids and physical barriers, such as cars parked on the pathway, the placement of furniture in a classroom, lack of parking spaces, and kerbs. The picture is complex in that the needs of disabled people are diverse (for instance, the lack of kerbs is problematic for blind people). However, non-disabled norms take no account of such human diversity. Indeed, as Edmunds, the director of the Greater London Association of Disabled People, states: *"at present society is constructed to meet the needs of the minority of non-disabled, working, white people without children"* (1997: 5) and discriminates against many non-disabled as well as disabled people.

The ideology of normality is manifest in all the rules, regulations, patterns of behaviour, social organisation, and aids to daily living that marginalise disabled people from the mainstream of society. Institutionalised discrimination is experienced by disabled people when they encounter so-called "public" buildings, transport, and facilities which they cannot enter, cannot use, or have so-called "special" provisions and "special" backdoor arrangements.

Shops, "public" houses and restaurants, theatres and cinemas, sports and leisure venues, town halls and law courts – the list of inaccessible buildings is well known to many disabled people. Furthermore, inaccessible housing is a key barrier to "independent living". It has been estimated that a quarter of a million people with physical impairments are inadequately housed. There is much evidence too that many disabled people are excluded from many transport systems (Liberty, 1994).

Ideologies of normality and independence are inherent in the construction of environmental disabling barriers:

> *"Much architecture has been planned with a young adult, non-disabled male paradigm of humanity in mind. In addition, aspects of social organisation that take for granted the social expectations of performance and productivity, such as inadequate public transportation . . . communication systems that are inaccessible to people with visual or hearing impairments, and inflexible work arrangements that exclude part-time work or rest periods, create much disability."*
>
> ***(Wendell, 1996, 40)***

ATTITUDINAL DISCRIMINATION
Attitudinal discrimination refers to negative feelings, beliefs, and behaviours (including stereotyping) of non-disabled and disabled people towards disabled people, such as "does he/she take sugar?", staring, and over-protection.

"Attitudes" are complex. They are generally seen as having three aspects:

> 1. a cognitive component, that is knowledge and understanding of "disability" (this can include knowledge of terms such as impairment, disability, and handicap, and knowledge of medical conditions);
> 2. an emotional component, that is the feelings provoked by disabled people; and
> 3. a behavioural component, that is how people act and react towards disabled people.

Attitudes are complicated further because there is a loose connection between these three components. Our understanding, our feelings, and what we do about things do not necessarily relate closely to each other. Nevertheless, each of the components is seen to play a part in negative attitudes. A negative attitude to people with Down's syndrome might include a lack of understanding about the impairment, a fear of people with Down's syndrome, and a behavioural component such as name calling and negative labelling. Professionals, including those in the health, welfare, and education fields, are seen as possible contributors to such attitudes (Swain and Lawrence, 1994) in that they further a specific medical or individual model of disability.

Of the three components of attitudes the most commonly cited seems to be emotional aspects. Roush's (1986) statement is an example:

> *"Typical emotional reactions when seeing someone with a disability include guilt, fear, and pity, all of which are characterised by a general feeling of discomfort."*
>
> ***(p 1551)***

Barnes (1996) argues that it is impairment, rather than disability, that non-disabled people fear as impairment reminds non-disabled people of their own mortality.

Such prejudice has been written about by some disabled people themselves, including Morris (1993):

> *"Although overt hostility is not a common experience for most disabled people, it is yet the iron fist in the velvet glove of the patronising and seemingly benevolent attitudes which we experience. This is clear from the experiences of those of us who step out of the passive role which our society accords to us. In these situations we often have to confront dislike, revulsion and fear."* *(p.103)*

French (1996) states:

> *"These evaluations are based on the underlying values we hold which represent ethical codes and social and cultural norms; whereas beliefs represent what we know, values represent what we feel."* *(p 151)*

The literature by disabled people testifies time and again to what we regard as the most fundamental challenge to non-disabled people generally and those who work with disabled people in particular, and that is: for many disabled people disability is not a personal tragedy, but may, on the contrary, enhance life or provide a life-style of equal satisfaction and worth (Swain and French, 1997). The following are a couple of examples, from many we could have chosen.

> *"As a result of becoming paralysed life has changed completely. Before my accident it seemed as if I was set to spend the rest of my life as a religious sister, but I was not solemnly professed so was not accepted back into the order. Instead I am now very happily married with a home of my own."* *(Morris, 1993: 120)*

> "...I cannot wish that I had never contracted ME because it has made me a different person, a person I am glad to be, would not want to have missed being and could not relinquish even if I were 'cured'."
>
> *(Wendell, 1996: 83)*

Yet the dominant view of disability in our society is that it is a personal tragedy. The policies, practices, and intervention of non-disabled people are justified and rationalised by the non-disabled view of personal tragedy. The tragedy is to be avoided, eradicated, or non-disabled (normalised) by all possible means. As Wendell states:

> "This is reflected in the assumption that potential disability is a sufficient reason for aborting a foetus, as well as in the frequent statements by non-disabled people that they would not want to live if they had to use a wheelchair, lost their eyesight, were dependent on others for care, and so on."
>
> *(1996, 54)*

Such are the negative presumptions held about impairment and disability that the abortion of impaired foetuses is barely challenged. The erroneous idea that disabled people cannot be happy, or enjoy an adequate quality of life, lies at the heart of this response. The disabled person's problems are perceived to result from impairment rather than the failure of society to meet that person's needs in terms of appropriate human help and accessibility.

Constructing Institutionalised Discrimination

In this section we have touched on some of the barriers that deny disabled people access to organisations. In understanding the construction of institutional discrimination, it is important to recognise the integral nature of the wall. Segregated education, inaccessible transport, inaccessible "public" buildings, unemployment, and underemployment all reinforce each other and are cemented through ideologies of normality and independence. Furthermore, from the viewpoint of disabled people, help in its various forms of charity, welfare, and professional intervention can itself be part of the SEAwall. Wendell expresses this succinctly:

> *"Disability is also socially constructed by the failure to give people the amount and kind of help they need to participate fully in all the major aspects of life in the society..."*
>
> ***(1996, 40)***

Disabled writers have consistently argued that such participation begins essentially with disabled people having control over the kind and amount of help they receive. Lack of control underpins enforced dependency, and is particularly marked in the lives of disabled children who are usually under the control of non-disabled adults who do not fully comprehend their needs (French, 1993b). In the next section we focus our model of analysis on professional help. We shall concentrate mainly on social work, but in general terms our analysis is applicable to all types of professional help.

Analysing professional practice: social work

The Context

In order to analyse institutional disablism we have chosen to focus on social work. In order to do this it is necessary to draw some distinctions about social work itself.

Social work as an activity is carried out in a variety of organisational settings and can describe a huge range of practices undertaken by workers who may or may not possess a professional qualification in "social work". Social workers are not autonomous professionals but employees of often large, bureaucratic organisations such as local authority social services departments, where they represent a very small percentage of the workforce (2% in most local authorities). Social work, as a profession, has "colonised" certain areas of activity in its drive towards professionalism (Hugman, 1991, Oliver, 1996). The assessment of the "needs" of disabled people is one such area (Middleton, 1997).

Social work as a profession has a history, and an ideology, that are thoroughly bound up with dominant discourses in society, such as the control of deviance, the maintenance of self-sufficiency, and the promotion of empowerment. Social workers are invested with power by the State on the basis of professional knowledge gained through State-approved, competency-based training. Examination and deconstruction of the elements which go to make up the institution of social work, such as education and training, ideology and organisational structure, reveal that institutional disablism exists at the very heart of social work and is often cloaked in its most liberal discourses, particularly with the language of "empowerment".

Professional Practice and Institutional Discrimination

The 1980s and 90s have witnessed massive changes to the profession of social work. The imposition of a competency-based paradigm upon social work education and training, the attack upon its value base, and the permeation of market forces in the form of privatisation of services have all contributed to the devaluation and dilution of anti-oppressive practice. The drive toward the survival of social work as a profession has led to its "proletarianisation" (Derber, 1982), which Hugman describes as:

> "...the separation of ideological and technical control... In the growth of hierarchies the caring professions have maintained their technical autonomy at the expense of ideological control through the objectives of the employing agency. Technical control becomes unnecessary because in this process the goals of the professionals become subordinated to those of the organisation."
>
> *(1991: 81)*

The reorganisation of social work training in the 1980s saw the introduction of competency-based learning and assessment. Dominelli suggests that:

> "Competencies in social work are a set of highly technical, decontextualised practice skills which can be broken down into smaller and smaller constituent parts that can be carried out by personnel trained to a specified level."
>
> *(1996: 154)*

The following are consequences of competency-based training:

a. It fragments and reduces social interaction and social problems;
b. It reduces social work to a set of performance criteria;
c. The breaking down of competencies into smaller and smaller elements allows less-highly-qualified individuals to take on social work tasks for less pay. Those tasks have traditionally been associated with the provision of services to older people

> and those with disabilities (see, for instance, the different "levels" of assessment offered within the National Health Service and Community Care Act of 1990 (Middleton, 1997));
> d. There is less space for professionals to exercise flexibility, autonomy, or discretion within such ritualised and prescribed practice;
> e. It separates out various forms of oppression and adopts an individualistic approach. Individual workers and users of services address oppression only as it is experienced by an individual.

These structural changes to the education of social workers have implications for the kinds of service that disabled people receive. Such an approach reduces social work to a formulaic activity in which both the worker and the service user are disempowered.

Values which are central to the practice of social work have also been under attack, and accusations of "political correctness" within social work have resulted in a change in emphasis from social justice and anti-oppressive practice to an equal opportunities approach to discrimination. This is evident in the revised version of the DipSW (CCETSW 1995), which Vass asserts

> *"...curtailed references to anti-discriminatory and anti-racist practice and focused, instead, on an Equal Opportunities statement limited to four paragraphs. It redefined the purpose, knowledge, values, and skills of the profession."*
>
> *(1996: 3-4)*

These developments together with the introduction of competency-based training have led to the individualisation of problems and interventions. The individual approach to discrimination is antithetical to that of the social model of disability which promotes collective action against oppression and the fight for civil rights. Such moves in the development of the social work profession represent a serious threat to the goals of disabled people to work in partnership with social workers to combat institutionalised disablism.

Many disabled people have experienced institutional discrimination when attempting to gain entry to social work training (James and Thomas, 1996, Baron et al., 1996). Once qualified, some disabled social workers have had to overcome significant barriers to employment and promotion (French, 1994a). Much has been written about the institutionalised racism and sexism that excludes women and black people from the higher echelons of social work management. Hugman makes the point that the gendered and racist structures and relations found within the caring professions reflect and reproduce those which are found in the wider society. He goes on to say:

"Caring professions are embedded in the patriarchal social structures, reproducing relationships in which the power of men over women is sustained. This power is expressed in assumptions about and the realities of differential employment of women and men, enabling men to pursue hierarchical careers and leading to the dominance of men disproportionate to their numbers in caring professions as a whole."
(1991:180)

In contrast to the issues of institutionalised class discrimination, sexism and racism, very little has been written about the discrimination experienced by disabled professionals. In another volume in this series (French, Gillman, and Swain, 1997) we included a case study of Alan Dudley who is blind and a senior social worker. The barriers he faced, he told us, began in gaining access to training. This is compatible with the findings of French's study of the experiences of disabled health and welfare professionals. She concluded:

"A sizeable minority . . . had experienced some degree of negative discrimination either as a result of their colleagues' attitudes or lack of understanding. Most of these problems occurred when attempting to gain access to training and during training." **(1988, 584)**

CONSTRUCTING INSTITUTIONALISED DISCRIMINATION

In general terms, as demonstrated in the above discussion, the SEAwall of institutional discrimination within professional practice marginalises and excludes disabled people as both users and employees. As the case study of a social work team in Section Two shows in some detail, disabled people face structural, environmental, and attitudinal barriers in gaining access to services. Structural barriers are apparent in hierarchical power relations, with professional services for disabled people being associated with low status and the use of unqualified staff. Barriers at the environmental level include inaccessible buildings and the dominant use of written information, form filling, and report writing. Regulations such as being able to drive, working from the office, and doing night duty exclude many disabled people from the social work profession. Professionals' attitudes to disabled people are difficult to measure and there is conflicting research evidence (French, 1996). However, as French points out:

> *"It is disturbing to note that most research about disabled people has focused on impairment rather than on social and environmental barriers and has been conducted by non-disabled people"*
>
> *(1996: 162)*

The research reviewed by French thus takes no account of the espoused model of disability. Professional theories and models have traditionally taken an individual, tragedy view of disability, and there is some evidence that this is the dominant conceptual model for professionals. Summarising research undertaken in a multiprofessional context, Swain states:

> *"In essence, disability was consistently viewed as a condition of the individual. Sometimes this was stated explicitly, as by a physiotherapist:*
> *'I look on the disability as being the overall diagnosis... to me the children have got a disability, i.e. spina bifida, cerebral palsy, to me that's the disability. That's the underlying problem...'*

> Others were more circumspect. The doctor, for instance, stated:
>> 'I use the World Health Organisation classification of impairment, disability and handicap, and handicap is the social effect of the disadvantage suffered because of a person having disability which means a loss or an alteration of function due to impairment'
>
> It is still clearly evident from this classification that the individual young person is the source of the problem"
>
> *(1995: 198)*

Again, enforced dependency is integral to processes of institutional discrimination, reinforced by the ideology of normality. In an unequal relationship in which the professional is the "expert", attitudes are wielded through ideological power to control definitions of what is "normal", what is "appropriate and acceptable", and what is "the problem". Oliver is sceptical about recent changes in terminology:

> "The professional-client relationship can itself also be dependency creating, and indeed the very language used suggests that power is unequally distributed within this relationship. Recent attempts to address this problem through changing the terminology from 'client' to 'user' or 'customer', acknowledge that the problem exists but do little to change the structures within which these power relations are located"
>
> *(1993: 54)*

In understanding the SEAwall model of institutional discrimination, however, it is also important to recognise resistance. The wall is constructed in the social and structural relations between non-disabled and disabled people, and between professionals and clients, and is characterised by processes of resistance as well as deterministic processes. There is evidence that clients confront professional definitions of problems and assert their own definitions of their needs (Begum, 1996 and French, 1994b).

It is clear from the above analysis that social workers are also subject to constraints which strengthen psychological or individual methods of intervention, through ideologies in training, in working practices, staff shortages, underfunding, and the consequent reliance on crisis intervention. Nevertheless, there is also a long history of resistance and radical dissent from within social work itself.

> *"The challenge for social work is to deliver an appropriate non oppressive practice. This means making constructive accommodation of the lessons from the past while adhering to a set of core values without colluding with popular attempts, from a range of political perspectives, to undermine social work's professional development."*
>
> ***(Vass, 1966: 57)***

Boushel (1994) and Saraga (1993) promote clients' perspectives and the establishment of social work as an empowering rather than repressive service for clients. However, until social work as a profession can begin to address the structural inequalities and disablism within its own organisation it is difficult to see how bodies such as CCETSW can, with any integrity, make claims to a value base which includes anti-discriminatory practice.

Section two:
Six case studies

In this section we provide brief synopses of
organisations working with disabled people. We have
called them "case studies", though they differ
substantially from the form of documents that are
usually associated with this term. They are studies of
organisations rather than individual people, and they
are based on the views of those involved, collected
through interviews and documentary evidence. In
relation to this guide, these studies have two main
aims:

> 1. To provide an overview of the work of a sample of
>   organisations providing services for disabled people;
> 2. To analyse the organisations in terms of the model of
>   institutional discrimination developed in Section One.

We are not suggesting that this is a representative sample.
Indeed, it is beyond the scope of the guide to provide such
an overview. There are many obvious omissions, such as
day centres, group homes, and hospitals. We sought to
provide an array of organisations offering a diversity of
approaches to illustrate the use of the SEAwall model.

For a number of reasons, the evidence on which these
studies are based is restricted. A major limitation is the
lack of substantial evidence from clients of the various
services offered by the organisations. Nevertheless, four of
the studies are based on interviews conducted for the
purposes of the guide. The *Skills for People* study is based
on documentary evidence and interviews conducted
previously by one of the authors. The *Derbyshire Centre
for Integrated Living* study is based on documentary
evidence.

SIX CASE STUDIES

We have not space in this guide to provide details about the methods employed in collecting this information. However, it is important to state that each organisation was sent a copy of a draft of its case study for comments.

The studies are all written to a similar format. They each present first a descriptive account of the organisation, though recognising that this in itself is partial and interpretative, before moving on to a more directed analysis.

A local authority community care team

This case study describes a local authority community care team, which works with people over the age of 18 years who require assistance that falls within the remit of the NHS and Community Care Act. Team members include qualified social workers, social services officers (SSOs), a team leader, and occupational therapists who also work with other teams in the borough.

The role of the team is to carry out assessments of need within the community which includes the allocation of a range of domiciliary services such as home care workers who assist with shopping, dressing, and housework, day, residential, and respite care, and social work support. The team operates a "care management process" which the team leader suggests is

> *"...to carry out assessments within the community. To produce an assessment document which identifies the needs people have got and which they have a copy of and keep. And then produce a care plan which shows how those needs are going to be met, or sometimes not going to be met. We implement that care plan... monitor that care plan to see whether services are appropriate and then... review the care plan and make changes."*
>
> **(Dave)**

There is a much higher proportion of unqualified staff in the community care teams compared with that which exists in the child care and mental health teams. One member of the team commented:

> "There is quite a big emphasis on unqualified staff in these teams and I think it is changing even more so to that... Most of the short term workers are the SSOs and the long term workers are social workers, so I would agree that most of the time we try to put the cases where the skills are. It's often the case of whoever has time to do it and sometimes they are taking on things that are unseen. In an ideal world they may not have been asked to do that at all. The onus is often put on the worker to have to say 'I feel I'm unable to do this'. That is quite a big thing to have to admit."
>
> *(Ann)*

There is a degree of ambivalence in the team about the introduction of the care management system. Some of the criticisms include the erosion of the social work role, the reduction in staff coupled with the raised expectations of the public in relation to community care, and the restrictions imposed by assessment documentation. Another concern stems from the current emphasis on individual assessments and care plans which have restricted social work activity, such as representing the views of oppressed groups within the community.

> "We don't meet with groups as much as we used to and put forward their ideas. It is not seen as so much of a social work task now. The social work task is to assess people."
>
> *(Dave)*

Others in the team felt that service users do not understand the care plans that are drawn up by the professionals but are prepared to "sign anything" in order to get assistance or services. In addition, care plans are not produced in a form accessible to some visually disabled people. Ann made the point that although the team members had received training in producing care plans, the users had not,

> "...they won't know why we are writing something in here. They are going to have no idea. You get them signed and that means that they have agreed to it, but I think that people in that situation will often sign anything because they're pretty desperate, they want some services. I know that I often don't explain fully and if you ask people where their care plan is the majority don't know. I think it is about the professional side thinking you have to have a nice piece of paper."

The positive aspects of care planning identified by the team include the notion that it makes workers more accountable for what they write about service users, it directs the worker's attention toward certain aspects of a person's life and therefore respects other areas as private or irrelevant to the assessment, and it provides workers with clearer parameters around entitlement to assessment, assistance, and services.

There is no restriction on the size of workload carried by each worker but staff are encouraged to close cases or to pass them on to long term workers as soon as possible. Bombardment of work is managed by a priority system drawn up by the local authority. Cases are categorised according to these priorities by the team leaders. The team leader explains:

> "Priority one represents a case where the situation has collapsed, or is about to collapse imminently, and you are required to provide some kind of care package where they would be safe and secure in their own home and be fed, or provide them with residential or nursing care because their carer has become ill. Priority two is a situation which is going to break down and should be dealt with, in theory, within two weeks. Where a carer who is looking after someone is getting very stressed and other members of the family can't help you put in domiciliary services

> or provide residential care. Cases in priority one and two get done, because they have to be. Priority three is supposed to be dealt with within 20 days and it is where people could use some help: the classic is assistance with bathing – it may require a bath board and seat and rails. We all accept that they need that but it is not life and death, it is not urgent and you could have a sponge down anyway: its not me saying this you understand – but that's it, and priority four don't get done."

An example of a request that should be categorised as priority four is, according to Ann, "...*for equipment that would improve your quality of life*". Another could be a request for help with managing bills. Such requests should have been dealt with by the team prior to the introduction of the care management process. Dave commented:

> "Unfortunately, that is what we have to tell people and it's quite hard when you are not used to saying no to people."

The team were aware of recent changes in legislation to allow disabled people to receive direct payments so that they can organise their own personal assistance. Ann is currently working with someone who has requested direct payment.

> "I'm working with a case who is going to be one of the first to get direct payment but they [the local authority] are working on methods I think, of being able to manage it but they don't appear to be against it at all. The feeling from consumers has been that the majority don't want to take it on. I don't think it is going to be a lot of people who want that sort of control because they feel it is going to be too much bother. The biggest problem the council seem to have with it is, how do they monitor it? What's been spent and where? 'cos they've obviously got to do that."

The offices occupied by the community care team are not open to the public and personal callers are discouraged. The building is inaccessible to some disabled people and the staff were unaware of any potential employees who might have been prevented or discouraged from working there. However, Dave made the point:

> *"Although we have an equal opportunities policy, like most other authorities do, the whole system of applying and actually getting training for social work is against people with disabilities doing it. People say 'hang on, could they do their visits?'"*

Service users can contact staff by telephone but their initial requests for assistance must be made to a "customer service centre" in the borough. Some of these centres are not accessible to disabled people.

> *"They couldn't just arrive at the door and get in. It doesn't actually promote independence. In terms of people who can't see very well, many of the buildings are difficult to find. There are no signs up there that could identify this is the council office. You have to ask for that and even when you get into them, someone has to tell you where the queue starts and ends and you rely on people to tell you when the queue is moving."*
>
> *(Dave)*

Access to information about services is limited. Whilst some information is available to visually disabled people on audio tape, very little is available in braille or produced in large print. The borough does employ interpreters for deaf people but they are not easily accessible because they are so much in demand. Some of the staff in the team have expressed an interest in learning to sign but no offer of training has been forthcoming. Laura felt that the local authority was no longer interested in supporting requests for professional development per se but prioritised training needs that supported service delivery.

DISCUSSION

This case study illustrates many aspects of institutional disablism and oppression of disabled people at a variety of levels, as depicted in the SEAwall of institutional discrimination. At the structural level, the social support required by disabled people is regarded by the local authority as special needs rather than civil rights. Dominant discourses such as prioritisation and assessment of need are used by the workers to carry out the local authority's role of distributing scarce resources, and denying many disabled people resources needed to live an ordinary life. As can be seen from the case study, the local authority has imposed a system of prioritising need which ignores the rights of disabled people to receive assistance that would enhance their quality of life. Social workers can only respond to those situations which Ann refers to as "matters of life and death".

As noted by members of the community care team, the 1980s and 1990s have witnessed massive changes to the profession of social work and its organisational contexts (see Section One). They have contributed to the devaluation and dilution of anti-oppressive practice and the subordination of the profession's goals to those of the organisation (in this case the local authority). For example, as Dave pointed out, social workers are no longer allowed to represent the collective voices of disabled people in their community and professional practices/organisational procedures, such as individual care plans, prevent social workers from intervening at a community or societal level. Dominelli argues,

> "...instead of linking different elements of oppression and engendering organisational, societal and personal change... [the focus is on] what the individual worker and the individual user can do... a tinkering at the edges of oppression without changing its fundamental framework. The causes of oppression, the institutionalised and culturally legitimated forms through which it is maintained and reproduced to affect whole categories of people and not just individuals, are left untouched."
>
> *(1996: 170-1)*

The combination of the dominant discourses of competency-based training for social work and the introduction of an inflexible system of care planning and assessment has resulted in a fragmented and instrumental service for consumers. It has reduced social work to a set of performance criteria which does not allow workers to exercise professional autonomy or discretion within such ritualised and prescribed practice (Dominelli, 1996).

On the other hand, it could be argued that the diminution of professional power allows disabled people more freedom to organise their own care; the introduction of direct payments to disabled people is one example. Oliver and Zarb (1992) found that disabled people who received direct payments had more freedom to participate in employment and leisure activities of their choice. They could arrange to receive the kind of help they wanted at a time that would fit with their requirements and schedules. Such flexibility allowed disabled people to follow the lifestyles of their choice. The notion that personal assistance should be provided by trained and qualified personnel has also been challenged by disabled people.

> *"I'm not looking for professional qualifications, nurses are definitely out. I'm looking for people who are enthusiastic... I want to train them in my own way."*
>
> ***(Morris, 1991: 32)***

At the environmental level, disabled people are discriminated against on a number of fronts. Local authority reorganisation within the borough over the past five years has led to the dismantling of the old social services department into a number of "functions", community care being one of 15. In the past, service users had access to their local social services office. Now, the local offices are not open to the public and personal callers are discouraged. Social workers appear to have become distanced from their local community and these measures seem to be a way of managing bombardment of demand. Service users are expected to contact "customer services" if they require assistance, yet many of these offices are not accessible to disabled people, and are not staffed by employees who have awareness of disabling barriers. In addition, reorganisation has meant that much of the information about the location of services is out of date. Laura explained:

> "We get a lot of calls on duty where people have accessed five or six numbers for the information that they needed because there have been so many changes in procedures and departments over the past four years."

Information about services is not, on the whole, accessible to disabled people. Very little is available on audio tape and there is no brailling service. Copies of care plans are sent to service users but there is no attempt to make these accessible to visually disabled users, or to those with a learning difficulty.

It may be that many disabled people would be discouraged from applying for assistance by these barriers to accessing services, or they may be forced to rely on others to request assistance on their behalf. As Dave pointed out,

"...it doesn't really promote independence".

This case study demonstrates that the thinking of those who have the power to plan and implement policy (in this case, that of planners in the higher echelons of the local authority) is not influenced by an awareness of disabling barriers, or of practices that exclude and marginalise disabled people. Institutional disablism is embedded within such organisations and is evident in the design and implementation of policies that are based on the assumption that consumers are non-disabled.

This case study also highlights the environmental barriers experienced by disabled people who wish to work in such organisations, or who would like to train as social workers. Disabled adults are two and a half times more likely to be unemployed than non-disabled adults and the average wage for disabled adults in employment is just 72% of their non-disabled counterparts (Gooding, 1996 p 4). There is evidence to suggest that disabled people are denied access to higher and further education (Barnes, 1991, Etheridge and Mason, 1994). A recent study of the barriers to training for disabled social work students found that they experienced discrimination in relation to physical access to buildings, disabling attitudes of course staff and practice teachers, and disabling teaching and learning practices that marginalised or excluded them (Baron et al. 1996). James and Thomas (1996) argue that disablist culture permeates and influences both education and employment organisations. They go on to say that

> *"...there are subtle connections too between the culture of an organisation, especially in relation to its employment practices and its service delivery. It is doubtful that a lack of commitment to one will allow a full flowering of the other. This seems to hold good for both educational institutions and providers of social services."*
>
> *(1996: 45)*

This is evidenced in the community care team by the environmental barriers facing both users of services and potential employees who happen to be disabled.

Discrimination at an attitudinal level can be identified within this setting. Within the profession of social work, working with disabled people is not perceived as high-status work. Stevens observes:

> *"Where social workers have expressed a preference for work within particular client specialisms they have most often chosen to work with children or offenders or to do mental health work rather than work with elders or people with learning difficulties or a physical disability."*
>
> *(1991: 12)*

As the team leader observed, the staff in the community care team are perceived by their colleagues as *"...carrying less complex cases"*, a view that is disputed by the team members. Research also indicates that the proportion of unqualified staff in such teams is higher than those teams working with children and families (Burke, 1990) and that the career development opportunities and promotion prospects are also poor (James and Thomas, 1996). Others have noted that the workforce in these teams is predominately female, with a much higher proportion of men working in the "high profile" areas of child protection and mental health (Hugman, 1991; Dominelli, 1996). Here the dominant discourse of women as carers is inextricably bound up with the medical model of disability that perceives disabled people as in need of care.

These attitudes to disability are also reflected in the curriculum of professional social work training where disability issues are marginalised. In 1991, CCETSW expressed concern that:

> "...disability will be seen by courses as of marginal special interest because of the small numbers of students currently wishing to opt for work with disabled people."
>
> *(1991: 20)*

Recent research seems to suggest that this is the current state of affairs within Dip SW programmes (Baron et al., 1996; James and Thomas, 1996). Baron et al. found that all the Dip SW programmes in their survey allocated CCETSW's minimum requirement of two days to disability issues; however,

> "...the compartmentalisation of disability in the timetable led to tutors seeing it as having been 'covered', and therefore not an issue to be discussed in other aspects of the curriculum."
>
> *(1996: 370)*

It can be seen that within the profession of social work the SEAwall of discrimination operates at all three levels.

Skills for People

Skills for People **is not a self-advocacy group as such. They do not talk about themselves as a self-advocacy group because the group is not controlled solely by disabled people.** *Skills for People* **is a project or organisation of people, established in 1983, which has self-advocacy as its main guiding principle (Swain, 1993) and is a registered charity.**

The project aims to:

> - help people with learning and physical disabilities to speak up for themselves;
> - support people to have more of a say in their lives;
> - help people make friends and build relationships;
> - help people become more confident;
> - help people know their rights;
> - let people know about the challenges faced by disabled people.
>
> *(Skills for People, 1997)*

The day-to-day work at *Skills for People* is conducted by a small team of paid staff (five at present) and volunteers (approximately a hundred), including disabled people, the majority of whom are people with learning difficulties, professionals, and other supporters. The overall responsibility for the organisation is held by the trustees, half the board being composed of volunteers and half being members of the church which provides the building for the project. The Trustees ultimately control the finances, employment of staff, and general policy issues. The decisions about the daily work of the project are made by the programme committee, composed of volunteers, which receives monthly reports from the staff members and monitors the work of the project. Wright, the Project

Co-ordinator, writes:

> "Central to the philosophy of the organisation is the belief that people who have disabilities should be enabled to speak up for themselves. Within Skills for People, every effort is made to ensure that this happens and the work of the project is planned according to the agenda of the disabled people within the organisation."
>
> *(1995: 141)*

The main part of their work is the planning and running of courses. They have included: *Self-Advocacy or Speaking up for Yourself, Doing for Ourselves, New Ideas, New Choices* (for people who communicate without words, and their supporters); *Building Relationships; Aim Sky High* and *Young People Moving On*. In the year ending March 1996, 600 places were taken up on courses and groups run by *Skills for People*. *Moving On* was a series of courses and follow-up days in the early 90s for young people with learning difficulties and physical impairments. The courses were planned, presented, and evaluated by young people themselves in teams drawn from schools and colleges in the area. The overall aim was to help young people to speak up for themselves, and topics covered have included "rights and responsibilities", "making choices" and "listening".

The recorded evaluations of the planning teams emphasise the importance of collective identity and voice.

> "It gives students a chance to get together."
>
> "Planning it ourselves is important. It is our own and the teachers do not plan it for us."
>
> "We made our own rules. We sorted out our own problems... instead of getting someone to do it for us, like in school."

This has provided the context for personal empowerment.

> *"I know now that we all have our opinions and decisions that we have to make. That is why speaking up for yourself is important."*
>
> *"There was one time when I would not have been able to go into the office and ask for my money, but I do now."*

One of the members of staff told us:

> *"We found that important things happened when people went through a process of planning and putting on courses, the confidence they get, the feelings they got of having control over something, learning to speak for themselves. It's the process that's the important thing, giving people the chance to speak for themselves, organise something and learn through that process. The project isn't about providing a service. It's about involving people with disabilities in providing a service."*

As well as providing courses for disabled people, *Skills for People* has been involved in training professionals and staff. They have planned and run courses, usually related to self-advocacy, for residential care staff of hostels, day services, and group homes, as well as contributing to professional programmes such as Diploma in Social Work courses. All such training includes sessions led by disabled people. *Skills for People* have also produced a training package called *Speaking up for Yourself – How to plan and run courses that really help*. It is designed to be used by people with learning difficulties as well as non-disabled supporters. They have also been asked to find out the views of people with learning difficulties for various purposes, for instance to find out what users of health and social services think of the services they receive. As far as possible they do this by involving the users themselves in the research: deciding on the questions to be asked; carrying out the research; preparing and presenting the report.

Other work by *Skills for People* has included working with local self-advocacy groups including *Sunderland People First* and *Speak Out North Tyneside*. At the request of a local museum, a team of volunteers from *Skills for People* evaluated and reported on access to all parts of the building, information, and exhibits. Finally, they have run conferences and consultation days, to discuss, for instance, Community Care plans.

A volunteer, who is a social worker, told us:

> "It's increased a lot people's self-confidence and more people are getting involved now. Skills is now really well respected by Newcastle Social Services, whereas before we were looked on with suspicion. They thought we were going to make waves."

This was reflected in interviews with senior social service managers conducted by Williams for the *Skills for People*'s 10th anniversary report:

> "Skills demonstrates another way; it stands out as a model."
>
> "There's never any debate about support for Skills – it's a top priority."
>
> **(Skills for People, 1994: 24.)**

Skills for People is also regularly used as a placement for trainees on social work training courses.

DISCUSSION

The orientation of *Skills for People* in confronting institutional discrimination has been through strategies of "changing minds". Volunteers, particularly people with learning difficulties, testify to the success of *Skills for People* from their point of view:

> *"It was brilliant! Everyone was treated the same and I felt really comfortable. Every week I went I got better and better and was not so agitated."* **Suzie Fothergill**
>
> *"I have got a lot more confidence in myself through being involved with Skills. I am more confident about telling people what I want. I have made lots of friends over the years I have been involved with Skills."* **Kevin Pringle**
> *(Skills for People, 1994: pp 16 and 21)*

In the same document, however, there is a single more-negative quotation which indicates the limitations of the approach taken by *Skills for People*. Jackie Beard, a woman with physical impairments, states: "I think that *Skills for People* is working more with people with learning difficulties and sometimes I feel out of it" (p 21). *Skills for People* does not explicitly espouse a social model of disability, and is not in any clear sense part of the Disabled People's Movement. There are links with local self-advocacy groups, that is groups of people with learning difficulties, but no other involvement with groups of disabled people. This, perhaps, reflects the broader relationship between people with learning difficulties and the Disabled People's Movement. Campbell and Oliver write:

> *"People First joined the BCODP in 1994. Both organisations are going through a tremendous learning curve, and tensions, due to prejudices and historical oppression, still run high."*
> *(1996: 97)*

As evident in this case study, there are inequalities even within the work of *Skills for People*. The Trustees, none of whom are people with learning difficulties, are responsible for financial decisions. It has to be said, however, that it is only in recent years that people with learning difficulties have been able to become charity trustees. Another example comes from the involvement of some volunteers as members of various services management committees in the region. As one volunteer explained:

> "On the Voluntary Organisations Council I'm just a token. I'm very unhappy about that situation and I talked to the general secretary about it. I keep getting reassured that I'm not a token, but she doesn't see the way people treat me. I try to get my opinion across, but I'm not listened to. They've never had anyone with a learning disability on their management committee before, so they've got a long, long way to go."

The building used by *Skills for People* is a disused vicarage which has been made accessible, though for instance the ramp to the front door is too steep to be negotiated by a wheelchair-user without help. There are to be major changes at *Skills for People*, however, as they have been awarded a substantial grant by the Lottery Commission. They will be acquiring their own building which they will be able to design to meet their own requirements. They are most likely, however, to retain the general approach they have developed over the past 14 years which helped them secure the funding. Despite the aims of *Skills for People*, institutional discrimination relating to all three levels of the SEAwall of discrimination is still in evidence.

Herefordshire Lifestyles

Herefordshire Lifestyles **was founded in 1985 in the city of Hereford. It started as a pilot scheme involving 12 disabled people but now works with over 150 people at any one time. In 1991** *Herefordshire Lifestyles* **became a registered charity and a company limited by guarantee. Disabled and non-disabled people work as equal partners within the organisation and on the board of trustees.**

The aim of *Herefordshire Lifestyles* is to enable every disabled person in Hereford to live a life of his or her choice. They state:

> *"All people are entitled to the means to achieve a good quality of life, with opportunities unhindered by barriers and inadequacies due to ignorance, prejudice and discrimination."*
>
> ***(Herefordshire Lifestyles, Annual Report, 1996)***

Herefordshire Lifestyles is dedicated to enabling individual disabled people to fulfil their aims and ambitions in any area of their lives whether it be a trip to the local shop or embarking on a new career. One-to-one support, mainly by volunteers, is provided where the person seeking assistance is always in control. The organisation promotes what it called a "blank sheet of paper" approach where people listen and respond to the aspirations of disabled individuals and provide one-to-one assistance. They state:

> *"From the outset the principal activity has been to encourage, enable and, if appropriate, arrange the necessary training for disabled people to achieve the personal goals they have set themselves, sometimes against formidable odds."*
>
> ***(Herefordshire Lifestyles, Annual Report, 1996)***

Herefordshire Lifestyles has a national reputation for its innovative, pioneering approach and is rapidly expanding; in recent years Lifestyle organisations have been developed in 12 other British cities and interest is spreading to continental Europe. Part of the work of *Herefordshire Lifestyles* is to support this expansion.

Herefordshire Lifestyles is committed to responding to requests for assistance from individual disabled people. These requests might concern accommodation, education, finance, health, mobility and transport, personal care, sport, social and leisure activities, training, and employment. Joan, a participant we interviewed, explained:

> "I was introduced to Jenny, my volunteer, and when I came out of hospital I went to the technical college and did a computer course. I think the most important thing is that anything I've wanted to know they've found out for me, and it's not always a case of doing it for you but enabling you to do it for yourself... When I found out that I would have to use the wheelchair I thought 'well, that's it, I'm just going to have to sit at home now and do nothing' but they raised my confidence a lot, I thought 'yes, I can do these things'. The biggest difference I've noticed is that my children could always find me at home, Mum was always in. Now they say, 'This is ridiculous, I'll have to make an appointment with you!'"

The help is provided in accordance with the wishes of the disabled person. Requests are never taken from relatives, carers, or organisations. Veronica, who works for the organisation, explained:

> "The main philosophy is that people are in charge of their own destiny. It's the disabled person that we are concerned with. It's what they want to do and where they want to go. And sometimes when they come here it's the first time that somebody has really concentrated on them and what they want."

Paid workers and volunteers can accompany disabled people, on a one-to-one basis, to any local venue or event of the disabled person's choice; for example the pub, an evening class, the local shop, or a hospital department. This assistance may be reduced as the disabled person becomes more confident. Joyce, who has received support from *Herefordshire Lifestyles* and now works as a volunteer, and trustee, explained:

> *"I talked about how I used to love dancing and they said to me, 'Well, why don't you go again?' So they found me a volunteer who took me to a dance club and the first night I was there I met somebody who I used to know 40 years ago and she picks me up every week and I've been going ever since... I also took up swimming lessons. These are things I'd never done... I really thought my life was finished when I became disabled. It raises your self-esteem and your confidence... You tend to feel that the world belongs to the able-bodied people and you have to take a back seat all the time and it makes you get up and go."*

It is recognised that people's goals and ambitions are varied and change over time. The organisation aims to be flexible enough to respond appropriately. This is achieved by very flexible working hours and allowing staff to respond to needs as they arise. Heather, who works for the organisation, said:

> *"We work a given number of hours and we decide what is the most appropriate use of that time and that's guided by what people want... It works in our favour too because we can be flexible, as long as we cover the hours by the end of the week it doesn't matter."*

Herefordshire Lifestyles liaises closely with over 70 organisations and is dependent on co-operative partnerships with them. These include statutory bodies, such as social services and the Health Service, voluntary organisations of and for disabled people, and commercial organisations. It is involved in many joint projects with these organisations some of which involve research. Rather than providing services directly, *Herefordshire Lifestyles* assists disabled people to access services which are available in the community.

The funding of the organisation is always precarious. In 1996 it was expecting a grant from social services and funding from the European Social Fund. Neither materialised, leaving the organisation with £35,000 less than anticipated. This has resulted in a reduction of staff hours. In fact, grants from social services have eroded over the years partly due to a mismatch of philosophy. Heather explained:

> "I think that the nicest referrals that we get... are the ones where they say, 'This person isn't doing very much in their life'... That is the nicest referral because we can then go with a totally clean page and start from what that person wants, not from what the social worker has assessed as being needed. That is so much better, but we are beginning to get far more defined requests... If it goes on like this we may decide that we don't want the contract from social services."

And Elaine said:

> "They tend to want us to take somebody somewhere where they 'ought' to go rather than seeing that we could have a much wider involvement. Somebody could choose to use us in other ways... Others see the value of what we do and try to work the system within their departments so that we can do it."

Funding has also become more specific to particular disabled people. Heather explained:

> "In the early days of Lifestyles we had funding that covered 'disabled people' whereas now it's much more specific. We have to give details about the numbers of people, ages, where they live and all that sort of business to attract funds. It's a lot less easy than it used to be."

Over the years money has been granted from many statutory, voluntary, and private organisations. In 1996 a grant was received from the National Lottery Charities Board and the Department of Health. The Rural Development Commission and Abbey National provided money for computer equipment, and a grant was received from The Foundation for Sport and Art. Money was also received from Scope and many small organisations as well as from individuals.

Herefordshire Lifestyles operates within a framework underpinned by the social model of disability. It is recognised that the barriers disabled people face lie within society and that these barriers must be dismantled if disabled people are to live the lives of their choice and to secure their full citizenship rights. The organisation aims to help disabled people gain the knowledge and find the strength to dismantle barriers themselves.

Joyce said:

> *"When you've done something that you've never done before it's a wonderful feeling of achievement... I used to think, 'There's nothing I can do, I can't sew, I can't read, I can't go out'. You get to the stage when you think there is nothing at all that you can do. But there are plenty of things you can do and do well. I do more now than I've ever done before and that's what keeps you alive really, isn't it? – the stimulation and the interest."*

Discussion

The aim of *Herefordshire Lifestyles* is to respond to the aspirations and goals of individual disabled people. To achieve this many of the structural barriers present in most organisations as depicted in the SEAwall have been dismantled. People who are employed by the organisation are given the freedom to use their working hours flexibly and initiative in responding to individual needs and goals. The differences in power between disabled and non-disabled people, so often seen in other organisations, have also been eroded. Disabled people, whether participants, volunteers, or employees, are treated equally. Joyce explained:

> "I was amazed when Len asked if I would be a trustee because I didn't think that people like me sat on boards. I really thought that it was a big joke and I said 'are you serious?' I always thought it was business people, smart people with loads of money and power."

Herefordshire Lifestyles does, however, work with and is dependent upon many other organisations who do not fully share its philosophy. This, as we have seen, can lead to problems with working relationships and funding.

Some of the environmental barriers disabled people commonly face have been removed in the offices of *Herefordshire Lifestyles*. Information produced by the organisation is, for example, put on audiotape, and Joyce, who is visually impaired, has adapted computer equipment to use in the office. Access to the building is not, however, ideal for people with motor impairments. Heather said:

> "The main entrance in the front is pretty hard for anyone who is a wheelchair user to get through and then there's another door. It's not the easiest of buildings to get into. I think if our office was anywhere other than at the front of the building it would be a problem but we generally see somebody who is trying to get in... but it's not ideal."

A compromise has been reached over access as the building is ideally situated on the High Street and is rent free. It is, however, impossible for many people with motor impairments to get upstairs which can lead to a lack of privacy as the downstairs office is busy.

Herefordshire Lifestyles works within the community to help and empower disabled people to bring about changes themselves. This is in contrast to many traditional health and welfare services which are restrictive and lead to dependency. The organisation has, however, been criticised for not campaigning for the rights of disabled people. Heather believes this is through:

> "...a lack of understanding of where our viewpoint is with the individual, if they want us to do something we will help them to do it. If they want to campaign and go on a demonstration we will help them to do it, but it is not our role to make these decisions, particularly as I am not disabled. I need to be guided by individuals to do what they want me to do. We will do anything provided it is not illegal."

The ethos and philosophy of the organisation, the large number of disabled people in positions of control, and the working arrangement within the organisation have all contributed to appropriate attitudes and behaviour towards disabled people. Joan explained:

> "They're always there but they don't force you into things, they don't push. There is no 'you've got to do this' or 'you ought to do this'."

Joyce agreed:

> "They don't tell you what you need. They talk to you, and then they might make suggestions, and they might come up with things that you've never thought of that you feel really keen to do."

Sirdar Road Primary School

Sirdar Road Primary School in south London was built in 1932 in the middle of a large council estate which is now half owner-occupied. It is a functional, rather ugly building which is largely on one level. There are 360 children in the school when it is full and their ages range from 7 to 11 years. Approximately half the children are from ethnic minorities.

There are only two disabled children in the school both of whom have hearing impairments. No physically disabled children attend even though the school is built on one level. Their inclusion may be inhibited by the presence of a special school for physically disabled children nearby. Similarly most visually impaired and hearing impaired children are educated in special units within the borough. The school has a considerable number of children who are loosely defined as having 'problems of learning' but who are not classified as 'disabled'.

This case study is based upon an in-depth interview with Gill, a teacher who works at the school.

Various institutional adjustments are made for the children defined as having 'problems of learning'. They are, for example, taught in smaller groups wherever possible and given extra time. The two children with hearing impairments have *Statements of Special Educational Need* and receive special provision in the form of extra adult help and equipment, largely from outside the institution. Gill explained:

> "In terms of learning difficulties the tack is always to throw whatever resources you have at it. When it comes to sensory disability then the tack is always 'What can we get in the way of equipment and extra help?' If Lucy, who is deaf, has her radio-microphone and somebody with her for 10 hours a week that is fine because it brings her to the curriculum. If the asthmatic children have their medication and their pumps and whatever, that

53

> *is sorted out and it is kind of expected that everything will run on wheels. But definitively it is the ones with learning difficulties that we consider our responsibility. That is because schools are learning institutions and every child is entitled to the National Curriculum."*

Children with a Statement of Special Educational Need are legally entitled to extra assistance and resources. Statements are, however, only allocated to a very select few with the initiative nearly always coming, not from the school, but from those parents who understand their value. Gill explained:

> *"Children are never statemented as an initiative from the school, only from parents. Councils don't like paying out the money for equipment and extra personnel. There are a lot of children who don't get as much as they should."*

Disabled children who do not have statements sometimes have *Individual Educational Programmes* but, in Gill's experience, these are often very sketchy because teachers *"know they do not have the time, the chance, the opportunity, the resources to do anything"*. Gill believes that the conditions in which she and her colleagues work make it difficult to accommodate disabled children. There are 30 children in each class and the National Curriculum is demanding. Resources are scarce and there is no interest in disability from senior staff. Rigid institutional rules also make it difficult to accommodate ill or disabled children. Gill related one example of a girl with leukaemia:

> *"I wanted to get her moved to a more convenient classroom where she wouldn't have to walk so far because she was very, very ill. Now for the purpose of the institution the classrooms are put in blocks; all the third years together, all the second years together, and so on. So they said, 'No, I don't think we can have one class three here and one there'. So I said, 'Well, can't we move the whole lot then?' But somehow it was considered that this would be too much to ask of an institution, to move half of its children for the sake of one child."*

Gill believes that life in the school is so organised around rules that nobody thinks to adapt them for disabled children even when this is possible.
She explained:

> "Half the time it just needs someone to think about it in a busy day. Children often don't ask because they are so used to the system that they think it is God given, they don't think things are movable at all. If nobody thinks, asks, or notices it can be very rigid."

Schools are also hierarchical organisations which makes it difficult for teachers to initiate even minor adaptations.

Staff education on disability at Sirdar School is sparse and is largely delivered by non-disabled "experts". There is no comprehensive Disability Equality Training provided and parents of disabled children do not have easy access to teachers. Gill believes that staff have little knowledge about disability and that this, together with their working conditions, can lead to frustration and negative attitudes. She explained:

> "They don't have a lot of knowledge. I would describe their attitude... they are sympathetic, they are not uncaring but they become very frustrated when the teaching and learning process is disjointed by something for which there is not the resources to make a bridge and then they can begin to sound very unsympathetic. It is because they are very frustrated with the system. It feels as if it is all down to them and they can't do anything about it. It's then that you hear people say 'I don't know what that child's doing in this school!' Really the teacher is feeling guilty because she can't get to grips with it. I think the negative attitudes are a reflection of that frustration."

There is nothing in the school's advertising brochure about disability or disabled children and nothing in the learning materials that the children use.

Gill stated:

> "I think if you came to my school, and it wouldn't be atypical, and you took a random selection from classroom books, textbooks whatever, you wouldn't find disabled people there. You would find the gender and race thing very much built in. If you picked up a maths book, for instance, that had pictures of people in, you would find black faces, Asian faces, girls and boys doing the same thing but you would never see anyone on crutches or in a wheelchair."

There are no disabled adults in the school apart from Gill herself who is visually impaired. Describing her own experience she said:

> "In teaching you are always made to think that you shouldn't really ask other people to do things that you can't do unless you can give something back. You can do a swap, like I swap games because I can't do it, but if I can't swap it I have to do it. There is nothing built into the system for disabled teachers at all."

DISCUSSION

This account illustrates institutionalised discrimination operating at the three levels of the SEAwall of discrimination described in *Section one*. At the structural level there is a system of special education for disabled children which has been in place for many years. This serves to inhibit the inclusion of disabled children in mainstream schools and is built upon and sustains an ideology of segregation. It emphasises the "difference" and "specialness" of disabled children, when compared with their non-disabled peers, and in so doing locates disability within the individual rather than within the social system.

Although the architecture of Sirdar School is largely flat, it appears that institutionalised discrimination at the structural level has inhibited the inclusion of physically disabled children. A further instance of institutionalised discrimination at this level is the absence of disabled people in the curricula materials and the school's own promotional literature. This reflects the hierarchical power relations and structures within society which have given scant import to the concerns of disabled people and which, in many ways, denies their existence. This, in turn, may inhibit disabled children and their parents from seeking help because of the fear of being adversely labelled and stigmatised.

Providing disabled children with *Statements of Special Educational Need* is, in some respects, a way of reducing discrimination at the environmental level. The deaf child, Lucy, for example, was provided with special equipment and a helper for 10 hours per week. These statements are legally binding and, as Gill points out, councils are reluctant to initiate the statementing process because of the costs involved. The process of statementing does, on the other hand, perpetuate the idea that the assistance needed by disabled children is "special" and something that should be provided from outside. This, in turn, may inhibit change from taking place within the organisation thereby absolving it of responsibility. Gill explained:

> *"I've had a couple of days, for instance, when Lucy's radio-microphone was broken, and it meant that for two or three days I really had to be very sure that she knew what I was saying in class and what was going on. I had to think about where I was standing, I had to make sure she was looking at me and so on. Each of these things sounds very small but if you had to go on and on with it it would get very hard. If you have the equipment you don't have to think about it, you can pretend that it's solving the problem. The help is all to do with 'specialness', it's not built into the system at all."*

It is likely, of course, that Lucy would find the accommodation to her needs, which Gill describes, extremely useful even when her equipment was intact. But the absence of a culture and ethos where disabled children are valued and where disability is viewed as an ordinary part of life makes even seemingly simple changes problematic.

At the environmental level of institutionalised discrimination Gill points out that rules, regulations, norms, and professional practice can inhibit the inclusion of disabled children. Some of these regulations are difficult to change, for example the size of classes, but others can be changed more easily if the will to do so is present, for example moving a classroom to accommodate a disabled child. Decisions regarding the allocation of resources can also have an impact on how successfully disabled children are included.

At the attitudinal level Gill highlights the lack of interest in disability issues from senior staff, not only with regard to disabled children but also disabled teachers. There is no comprehensive Disability Equality Training provided at the school and most of the teachers lack knowledge about disability and disabled people which is exacerbated by the very low numbers of disabled children and staff in the school. Although their attitudes may be basically accommodating, it appears that the lack of support they receive, due to structural and environmental discrimination, together with lack of knowledge, leads them to become frustrated, unsympathetic, and unwilling to accommodate children whose needs are not regarded as standard.

Enforced segregation of disabled children into special schools can be regarded as a denial of human rights, not just in terms of education, but in terms of full citizenship within the community. It is likely that many teachers in mainstream schools support the struggle of disabled people against institutionalised discrimination even though the ethos and practice of their profession create so many barriers. Individual teachers are not helpless victims of the systems in which they work, and may succeed in effecting important changes for disabled children, but they are greatly hampered by inequalities which are built into the very fabric of educational organisations and provision.

Derbyshire Centre for Integrated Living

The *Derbyshire Centre for Integrated Living* (DCIL) was founded in 1985 as an initiative of the *Derbyshire Coalition of Disabled People* working in collaboration with Derbyshire County Council. It was the first centre for integrated living in Britain. The centre is modelled on centres for independent living in the USA which were established in the 1970s. An important difference, however, is that the DCIL, and similar centres in Britain, work in partnership with existing State welfare services such as the health services and social services.

The aim of the DCIL is to secure a full economic, public, and social life for disabled people in accordance with their own wishes and desired lifestyles. It exists to find ways of removing barriers which stand in the way of disabled people leading full and satisfying lives. The centre is run jointly by disabled and non-disabled people working in partnership.

The aims of the centre are based upon seven basic needs which have been identified by disabled people themselves. These needs, which all interact and must, therefore, be provided in an integrated way, are for: Information, Technical aids, Transport, Counselling, Housing, Personal assistance, and Access.

The DCIL maintains an up-to-date and comprehensive information base for disabled people, their assistants and service providers. It is also available to researchers. This data base of information is extensive including, for example, information on holidays with over 3,000 accessible venues. The first point of contact for enquirers is with a disabled person who has wide knowledge of disability issues as well as personal experience of disability.

A Minicom is provided so that hearing-impaired people can use the telephone and the information is also available in braille, large print, and on audiotape. A braille, large print, and computer consultancy service is available commercially to other agencies.

The DCIL has a team of trained peer counsellors who are mostly disabled themselves. This service provides support for disabled people who are feeling isolated or experiencing difficulties in areas such as sexuality or transition to independence. The counsellors bring their own experience of disability to the situation and are not shocked by sensitive subjects or feelings such as grief and anger.

The DCIL provides training which, though tailored to specific requirements, is based upon a thorough understanding of the social construction of disability. Training is provided for volunteers, counsellors, information workers, and local access and transport groups. A range of courses are offered on a commercial basis.

The *Derbyshire Centre for Integrated Living* provides personal support services and personal assistance. They state:

> *"DCIL supports the right of all disabled people to determine how, when, where, and by whom the services they need are provided"*
> *(Derbyshire Centre for Integrated Living: a profile of an organisation, undated).*

Personal assistance can be defined as help provided by other people to enable disabled people to live the lives they choose. Support may be needed in returning to work, going to college, coping with rehabilitation, or the onset of impairment. Each package of personal assistance is designed to meet the individual wishes and needs of the disabled person and is managed by, or co-managed with, the disabled person himself or herself.

The centre also provides a maintenance and repair service. This runs rather like the AA. The engineers are fully qualified and totally aware of the significance to disabled people when their equipment breaks down.

The *Derbyshire Centre for Integrated Living* works in partnership with many other organisations including *SCOPE, British Association for Counselling, Living Options Partnership,* and *The Consortium on Opportunities for*

Volunteering. Its aim is to highlight disabling practices and help develop more appropriate services for disabled people. DCIL participates in joint planning with health and social services ensuring that the personnel of these services understand the priorities of disabled people.

DISCUSSION

This case study was constructed from literature produced by DCIL. Although this method can be criticised (official documents are not always totally reliable) it appears that many of the barriers disabled people routinely face have been removed within the organisation. The building is accessible to people using wheelchairs – and braille, audiotape, and large print are all provided. The people giving information have a broad knowledge of disability issues not only in a professional sense, but in terms of personal experience. A counselling service is provided by disabled people who have first-hand experience of encountering and removing barriers which stand in the way of a fulfilling lifestyle.

The staff of DCIL work within the community, not simply to visit and help disabled people overcome problems, but to empower them to bring about changes themselves. This is in contrast to many of the traditional health and welfare services disabled people receive which are restrictive and lead to dependency. DCIL helps disabled people to find appropriate personal assistance, which is not controlling or patronising, to enable them to lead the lifestyles of their choice.

They state:

> *"In the past many disabled people have had services delivered to them which have not given them sufficient control over their lives, for example services which of necessity have had to conform to particular models of service provision into which disabled people had to fit... We offer a different approach. Because we believe that disabled people have the right to determine their own lives in every aspect, we offer a service that reflects this approach."*
> ***(Personal Support Service. DCIL. undated)***

The *Derbyshire Centre for Integrated Living* provides Disability Equality Training to its own staff and volunteers as well as outside agencies. Disability Equality Training, in contrast to disability awareness training, does not focus solely on attitudes but on every aspect of disabling barriers and institutionalised discrimination. This is to ensure that people such as volunteers understand the full extent of the barriers which disabled people face and that attitudes are seen within an historical and cultural context.

When services are provided to disabled people by large bureaucratic organisations, unacceptable delays are very common. There is often a lack of concern or understanding that disabled people are dependent on equipment, such as a wheelchair, a visual aid, or a car, to function adequately at work or to enjoy leisure pursuits. These delays are frequently underpinned by structural discrimination where disabled people are viewed as unimportant or where lack of resources makes delays inevitable. The repair and maintenance service removes the anxiety and frustration when equipment breaks down and helps disabled people remain active citizens on their own terms.

It is likely that, within the culture and ethos of DCIL, attitudes and behaviour towards disabled people are good, illustrating that attitudes are shaped by organisational philosophies and practices. Decision making and working practices within the organisation are controlled by disabled people who do not regard disability as an individualised tragedy but as a civil rights issue. Every aspect of the work is geared towards the fulfilment of disabled people on their own terms and in viewing disabled people as active, capable citizens who are restricted, not by impairment, but by a disabling society.

A GP practice

This case study is based upon a group interview with four members of staff at a GP practice in the north of England.

The practice is housed in a building which was erected in the early 1990s. It contains various physical features which are essential to disabled people, for example an adapted toilet and automatic doors, but many limitations were highlighted. There is no lift to the upper floor for example, and; although this does not affect patients and clients, it precludes the employment of disabled staff who cannot manage the stairs, and disabled colleagues from other institutions.

Pauline, the health visitor, recalled:

> *"We once had a lady from the community health council. She was in a wheelchair and she couldn't get up here. So disabled professionals are stuck I think."*

No disabled staff are, or have been, employed in the practice.

The fire doors also create a problem. Tom, the GP, explained:

> *"One thing, we've got fire doors on the consulting rooms which are quite heavy and that's quite difficult for people. I mean not just people in wheelchairs but people who are frail and elderly. But I don't think there's any way round that."*

Many of the disabling features of the building adversely affect non-disabled patients and staff as well.

A GP PRACTICE

Evelyn, the receptionist, explained:

> "The reception isn't very good even for able-bodied people because the desks are at a terrible height, with them standing on one side and us sitting on the other. There is a lower area for people who are in wheelchairs but it's completely out of the way, in the wrong place... so it doesn't get used. Also, it's a very noisy area and it's not very good for confidentiality."

The height of the couches also poses a problem. Angela, the practice nurse, said:

> "The difficulty I have is that if someone has to get from a wheelchair to a high couch, that it quite difficult for them because I'm usually working by myself... If they've got someone with them, a carer, they'll come in and help because they know how the person likes to be moved and what they can do."

The high couches also pose a problem for Tom and his patients and changes the way he works:

> "I think the difficulty is, with people in wheelchairs particularly, unless there's a good reason we tend not to examine them on the couch. This is not necessarily the best thing but it is the most practical thing really."

These problems could be solved by having adjustable couches.

The building also poses problems for disabled parents with young children. Pauline explained:

> "We have a problem in the clinic area. I can think of one lady who has a disability with a young child and all of our changing mats are up at a height, the scales are on a table, it's all designed for able-bodied people. She has great problems lifting the baby, she has to bring a relative in to give her a hand."

A GP PRACTICE

The staff have available to them a list of interpreters to assist communication with deaf people and Pauline and Evelyn have both attended evening classes to learn sign language which they financed themselves. Unfortunately, they do not get sufficient practice. Evelyn said:

> *"Anyone who came in who was deaf I used to say 'Do you sign?' and they would say 'No'. Then last week this deaf chap came in and I said 'Do you sign?' and he said 'Yes' and he started to sign away at me and I said 'Stop, I've forgotten it all'."*

Angela highlighted particular ways in which deaf people might be denied full access to the service:

> *"You might not pick up on the cues you get from people who are hearing. You know, how they come in with a sore throat and they want to talk about their marriage or whatever it is. With someone who is profoundly deaf you would just treat the sore throat... You wouldn't pick up the subtleties."*

Very little adaptation is made in the practice for visually disabled people though the practice leaflet has been transcribed into braille. Angela mentioned the hazards of the car parking area:

> *"It's horrendous. If blind people are using a stick there is nothing to guide them across from the pavement. There's a small path but they've still got to get over the car parking area and cars are always coming and going. And there's the bollards."*

People with learning difficulties are seen in the practice but no specific provision is made for them. Tom said that no service would be knowingly denied and that every person would be treated as an individual. There is a community learning disability team in the area and Angela, talking of routine health checks, felt that it might be better

A GP PRACTICE

if people with learning difficulties received such services from the specialist team:

> "Personally I would find it quite difficult. I mean people who are trained in dealing with learning disability they know exactly what level to pitch their communication. I find that quite hard to do. They were suggesting a nurse to do smears, blood pressure, and things like that, but if we've got a community learning disability team who are specialists, why not use them but perhaps bring them into the practice if we've got a room available."

DISCUSSION

Although this GP practice was built in the 1990s it has numerous disabling features which preclude many disabled people from working there and causes great difficulty for disabled patients and clients as well as the staff themselves. The building was designed without any consultation with the staff or with disabled people. Angela thinks it meets legal requirements but no more.

Some of the adaptations that have been made are useful but they can be regarded, overall, as tokenistic. An example of this is the single leaflet transcribed into braille. The practice has many other leaflets, regarding health education, which are not accessible to visually disabled people or people with learning difficulties. There is no information in large print or on audiotape even though only a fraction of visually disabled people read braille. Evelyn said,

"I've found this out – like most deaf people don't sign".

This illustrates many environmental barriers in the SEAwall of institutional discrimination.

Several examples of structural discrimination arose in this interview. Although the staff in the practice seem keen to provide disabled people with a quality service, they have not had the opportunity to attend Disability Equality Training and are forced to rely on "intuition" and "common sense".

A GP PRACTICE

Evelyn said:

> *"We do a lot of training but we've never done that kind of training. I think the girls are very intuitive, most of them have been in the job a long time, they're very good about picking up on people who can't read, for example, or filling in their forms. It has never come up and I've been here for 15 years. It's long overdue."*

There is no user involvement in the management and running of the practice. Tom tentatively justified this in terms of the non-representation of people who join committees:

> *"It has been muted obviously but we decided it wasn't really... I don't know how to put it... They're not representative of the population really, the usual sort of thing, the same sort of patients all the time."*

This argument for the exclusion of disabled people has been strongly rejected by disabled people. Oliver states:

> *"In representative democracies, representation is always less than perfect, the Conservative Party does not represent all Conservative voters, nor does the British Medical Association represent all doctors... And yet the right of the Disability Movement to represent disabled people is continually questioned by politicians, policy makers and professionals alike... If the legitimate claims of the movement to represent disabled people is denied, who else will represent our interest – doctors, politicians, the Royal Institutes and Associations?"*
>
> **(1996: 150)**

The issue of how far people with learning difficulties should be in mainstream health and social services is also a contentious one. Although there may be some advantages, as outlined by Angela, the existence of specialist services has the potential to create feelings of inadequacy and deficiency in other workers and goes against the philosophy of inclusion of disabled people in society. Sperlinger states:

> *"A significant number of GPs do not feel that they should have the lead responsibility for dealing with general medical problems of people with learning disabilities, but assert that it should be the role of medical staff from the specialist learning disability team… Studies consistently show that primary health care team members acknowledge that they have only minimal education on the needs of this client group, yet only a minority welcome the possibility of further training."*
>
> *(1997: 12)*

Treating people at home, as a solution to an inaccessible environment, can also deny disabled people the opportunity to participate fully in society, and treating people "as individuals", as a substitute for dismantling disabling barriers, is unlikely to bring about equality of service or full accessibility for disabled people.

Section three:

Enabling access

In this concluding section, we explore possibilities for change and breaking down the SEAwall of institutional discrimination.

Over the past approximately 20 years, the main force for change has increasingly come from disabled people themselves, with the growth of the Disabled People's Movement. The activities of the movement have been diverse and have challenged institutional discrimination at every level of our framework. The movement is essentially embodied in the formation of organisations run and controlled by themselves. As with other civil rights movements, the highest public profile has been achieved through non-violent direct action targeted, for example, at inaccessible transport in Birmingham and charity telethons. Disability arts represents another strand of activities within the movement (see below). Finally, though this summary is far from comprehensive, there has been a more academic strand to the activities of the Disabled People's Movement, with the growth of "disability studies", research, conferences, and publications generated by disabled people.

Two examples of organisations which are largely run by disabled people are explored in this guide (*Derbyshire Centre for Integrated Living* and *Herefordshire Lifestyles*). In these organisations, the voices of disabled people have been privileged over professionals' views about what constitutes "suitable" services and social support. Professionals have learnt to respect the expertise of disabled people in relation to their support needs and have been able to work in partnership with disabled people to help them achieve their desired lifestyles. Many social workers and other professionals who work with disabled people are employed by local authority social services departments similar to that which is described in this guide. They too can challenge institutional discrimination of disabled people by promoting and supporting such developments as the introduction of direct payments under the NHS and Community Care Act.

We shall concentrate here on strategies for changing policies, particularly the campaigns for anti-discrimination legislation, and strategies for changing attitudes, particularly Disability Equality Training and disability arts.

Changing policies

The campaign for civil rights legislation by disabled people and their supporters has a long history, both inside and outside Parliament, and has been the major strategy of the Disabled People's Movement in their struggle against institutionalised discrimination (Barnes, 1991 and Liberty, 1994). Essentially, this history dramatically illustrates the fundamental nature of institutionalised discrimination, as formulated in the SEAwall, and the concerted and collective efforts of a marginalised section of the population to break down discrimination.

Campaigns in many countries (notably the United States of America, Canada, and Australia) have led to full civil rights legislation. In the UK, political pressure culminated in the passing of the Disability Discrimination Act (DDA) in 1995. We shall focus here on the DDA, briefly summarising what it does and does not do, building on our analysis of institutional discrimination.

As we shall outline below, the provisions of the Act are severely restricted. It is, however, a complex Act with numerous caveats, and we can only indicate its general scope here. The Act, at least in principle, establishes new rights for disabled people in the UK in the areas of employment, the provision of goods and services, and buying and renting land and property. Employers are required to take "reasonable measures" to ensure that they are not discriminating against disabled people. Under the Act it is against the law to treat disabled people less favourably "unless there are good reasons" to do so. It will be against the law to refuse to serve a disabled person or to offer a service that is not as good as the service offered to other people. It will also be against the law for anyone who sells or lets land to "unnecessarily discriminate" against disabled people.

Despite the rhetoric of the DDA the campaign by disabled people for full civil rights has continued unabated. There are four main interrelated grounds of criticism.

1. Though the Act is ostensibly directed towards eradicating discrimination, the espoused definition of disability perpetuates the individual model of disability. It is geared towards the identification of individuals, equating individual impairment and functioning with disability. As Rights Now (undated) points out:
   > "What the law asks is: are you disabled enough by an impairment to deserve fair treatment? Not: are you disabled by discrimination" (p 9).

2. As a direct consequence of this orientation to defining disability, the Act includes some but also necessarily excludes others. The dominant discourse has remained firmly focused on the non-disabled "common sense" question of who is disabled, rather than addressing the barriers of institutional discrimination. The Act, for instance, excludes people who may be discriminated against because of their association with disabled people, such as the parents of disabled children.

3. The Act is piecemeal and restricted in scope, not only in terms of applying to some and not others, but also in applying to some areas of life and forms of discrimination, and not others. Unlike the sex and race discrimination laws, the DDA does not apply to firms employing fewer than 20 people. Education is excluded from the Goods, Facilities and Services section of the Act, and educational establishments are not required to make their facilities accessible. There are major loopholes too in requirements relating to transport and information (such as the provision of information in braille).

4. In terms of the legal protection provided against institutional discrimination, the Act is limited in at least two major respects. First, discrimination can be legally justified under this Act, unlike the sex and race discrimination Acts. The justifications are different under different sections of the Act, resulting in different definitions of discrimination. The definition of what constitutes a "reasonable adjustment" also

> differs according to the section of the Act. Even in its own terms, lack of clarity militates against effectiveness. Second, the Act "lacks teeth". There is to no enforcement agency for the Act, along the lines of the Equal Opportunities or Racial Equality Commissions, although this is under review. The Act sets up an advisory board, a National Disability Council. Its members are appointed by the Secretary of State and its role is solely to advise the Secretary of State on the operation of the Act and on the elimination of discrimination. It has no power to investigate individual complaints, cannot provide assistance or advice to complainants, and has no powers of enforcement.

This Act is so weak that it is unlikely to bring about any effective change as it stands. It is possible, however, that with pressure from disabled people it will gradually be strengthened, although many people believe that it is so flawed that it ought to be completely scrapped rather than ammended (Trade Union Disability Alliance, 1997). The most effective role for professionals is to join disabled people in their struggle for fully comprehensive civil rights legislation.

Changing minds

The traditional approach to changing attitudes, often under the guise of "disability awareness training", has been geared towards changing the emotional dimension, to develop ostensibly positive responses of acceptance and sympathy, often including fact sheets about incidence of impairment, "medical conditions" and so on, to foster "understanding".

The Disabled People's Movement has rejected this approach. The main orientation has been to disseminate and promote a social model of disability, rather than feelings towards disabled people, as clearly expressed in the aims of Tyneside Disability Arts (TDA):

> *"TDA recognises that disabled people are disabled not by their own impairments but by the environment within which they live: by the social, cultural and economic barriers that obstruct their attainment of full rights to be recognised and involved as equal partners within a democratic society. Through the promotion and development of Disability Arts within Tyneside, TDA aims to address this issue and to achieve the inclusion of disabled people within Tyneside life Through TDA disabled people are able to use art in order to express the lived experience of disability as a lived experience of social exclusion and oppression; and by doing so, to further the struggle against this exclusion and oppression"*
> *(TDA, 1997, 4)*

The roots of Disability Arts lie in the politicising of disability issues. As Shakespeare, Gillispie-Sells, and Davis state:

> *"Drama, cabaret, writing and visual arts have been harnessed to challenge negative images, and build a sense of unity*
> *(1996, 186).*

The activities are so diverse it is difficult to talk in general terms. However, Vic Finkelstein, who was one of the founders of the London Disability Arts Forum (LDAF) in 1987, stated in his presentation at the launch that his hopes for the future were *"disabled people presenting a clear and unashamed self-identity"*. He went on to say that it was *"essential for us to create our own public image, based upon free acceptance of our distinctive group identity."* (Campbell and Oliver, 1996). This development of identity has indeed been central to disability arts, challenging the values that underlie institutional discrimination. Through song lyrics, poetry, writing, drama, and so on, disabled people have celebrated difference and rejected the ideology of normality in which disabled people are devalued as "abnormal". They are creating images of strength and pride, the antithesis of dependency and helplessness.

Another way in which the Disabled People's Movement strives to change disabling attitudes is through the development of 'Disability Equality Training' (DET). In its strictest sense Disability Equality Training refers to courses delivered only by tutors who have been trained by organisations of disabled people, in particular the Disability Resource Team and the Greater Manchester Coalition of Disabled People. These organisations train disabled people themselves to be trainers. The courses are not about changing emotional responses to disabled people but about challenging people's whole understanding of the meaning of 'disability'. The following are the stated aims of courses run by disabled trainers who have themselves been trained through the work of the Disability Resource Team:

> *"A DET course will enable participants to identify and address discriminatory forms of practice towards disabled people. Through training they will find ways to challenge the organisational behaviour which reinforces negative myths and values and which prevents disabled people from gaining equality and achieving full participation in society."*
> **(Gillespie-Sells and Campbell, 1991: 9)**

This form of training is endorsed by CCETSW who actually published the Trainer's Guide (Gillespie-Sells and Campbell, 1991). However, there is little evidence to suggest that there is any commitment to Disability Equality Training within DipSW training itself (Baron, 1996). In addition, our case studies suggest that Disability Equality Training is not offered to social workers, health care staff, teachers, and clerical staff on an in-service basis either. In the case study which discussed the work of a community care team, the staff had received "equal opportunities training" which was designed to raise awareness of impairment and other forms of difference. This kind of training is rejected by the Disabled People's Movement on the grounds that it promotes sympathy and pity and uses methods which attempt to simulate impairment and disability in a disrespectful and unhelpful way.

In conclusion, we have examined the approaches and strategies adopted by the Disabled People's Movement to challenge oppression and discrimination at all three levels of our SEAwall model and to promote change. The most insidious forms of discrimination are to be found within organisations whose very structures and procedures marginalise and exclude disabled people.

Professionals, and all who work with disabled people, need to become informed about disability in its widest sense and about the many factors which constitute institutional discrimination from adverse attitudes and behaviour to structural inequalities and poverty. Such an understanding can, to some extent, be achieved through professional education and a non-disabling ethos within professional organisations. The dismantling of institutional discrimination is such, however, that professionals working towards this goal on their own are unlikely to succeed. Dismantling institutional discrimination is a major political enterprise which involves enormous energy and struggle. The authors invite readers to join forces with the Disabled People's Movement and to use their professional power in collaboration and partnership with disabled people to dismantle every aspect of the SEAwall of discrimination and to liberate disabled people.

References

Barnes, C. (1991) *Disabled People in Britain: A case for anti-discrimination legislation*, Hurst and Company, London.

Barnes, C. (1996) Theories of disability and the origins of the oppression of disabled people in western society. In Barton, L. (ed), *Disability and Society: Emerging Issues and Insights*, Longman, London.

Baron, S., Phillips, R., and Stalker, K. (1996) Barriers to training for disabled social work students, *Disability and Society*, 11, 3, 361-77.

Beardshaw, V. (1988) *Last on the List: Community services for people with physical disabilities*, King's Fund Institute, London.

Begum, N. (1996) Doctor, doctor... Disabled women's experiences of general practitioners. In Morris, J. (ed), *Encounters with Strangers: feminism and disability*, The Women's Press, London.

Boushel, M. (1994) The protective environment of children. Towards a framework for anti-oppressive, cross cultural and cross national understanding, *British Journal of Social Work*, 24, 173-90.

Burke, P. (1990) The fieldwork team response: an investigation into the relationship between client categories, referred problems and outcome, *British Journal of Social Work*, 20, 469-82.

Campbell, J. and Oliver, M. (1996) *Disability Politics: understanding our past, changing our future*, Routledge, London.

References

Central Council for Education and Training in Social Work (1995) *Assuring Quality in the Diploma in Social Work: rules and requirements for the Dip SW*, Central Council for Education and Training in Social Work, London.

Davis, L. (1995) *Enforcing Normalcy: Disability, deafness, and the body*, Verso, London.

Derbyshire Centre for Integrated Living (undated) *Derbyshire Centre for Integrated Living: a profile of an organisation*, Derbyshire Centre for Integrated Living, Ripley.

Derbyshire Centre for Integrated Living (undated) *Personal Support Services*, Derbyshire Centre for Integrated Living, Ripley.

Dominelli, L. (1996) Deprofessionalizing social work: anti-oppressive practice, competencies and postmodernism, *British Journal of Social Work*, 26, 2, 153-75.

Drake, R.F. (1996) A critique of the role of the traditional charities. In Barton, L. (ed) *Disability and Society: Emerging Issues and Insights*, Longman, Harlow.

Edmunds (1997) Disabled people are trying to overcome society's barriers, *letter to Therapy Weekly*, 24, 4, 5.

Etheridge, D. and Mason, H. (1994) *The Visually Impaired: Curricular Access and Entitlement to Further Education*, David Fulton, London.

Finkelstein, V. (1993) Disability: a social challenge or an administrative responsibility? In Swain, J., Finkelstein, V., French, S. and Oliver, M. (eds) *Disabling Barriers – Enabling Environments*, Sage, London.

French, S. (1988) Experiences of disabled health and caring professionals, *Sociology of Health and Illness*, 10, 2, 170-88.

French, S. (1993a) What's so great about independence? In Swain, J., Finkelstein, V., French, S., and Oliver, M. (eds) *Disabling Barriers – Enabling Environments*, Sage, London.

French, S. (1993b) 'Can you see the rainbow?': the roots of denial. In Swain, J., Finkelstein, V., French, S., and Oliver, M. (eds) *Disabling Barriers – Enabling Environments*, Sage, London.

French, S. (ed) (1994a) Disabled people and professional practice. In French, S. (ed) *On Equal Terms: Working with disabled people*, Butterworth-Heinemann, Oxford.

French, S. (ed) (1994b) *On Equal Terms: Working with disabled people*, Butterworth-Heinemann, Oxford.

French, S. (1996) The attitudes of health professionals towards disabled people. In Hales, G. (ed) *Beyond Disability: Towards an enabling society,* Sage, London.

French, S. (1998) Surviving the Institution: Working as a visually disabled lecturer in higher education. In Malina, D. and Maslin-Prothero, S. (eds) *Surviving the Academy: women's experience of higher education*, Taylor and Frances, London.

French, S., Gillman, M., and Swain, J. (1997) *Working with Visually Disabled People: bridging theory and practice*, Venture Press, Birmingham.

Gillespie-Sills, K. and Campbell, J. (1991) *Disability Equality Training: Trainers Guide*, Central Council for Education and Training in Social Work, London.

Gooding, C. (1996) *Blackstone's Guide to the Disability Discrimination Act 1995*, Blackstone Press, London.

Herefordshire Lifestyles (1996) *Annual Report*, Hereford.

Hugman, R. (1991) *Power in Caring Professions*, Macmillan, Basingstoke.

REFERENCES

James, P. and Thomas, M. (1996) Deconstructing a disabling environment in social work education, *Social Work Education*, 15, 1, 34-45.

Liberty (National Council for Civil Liberties) (1994) *Access Denied: Human rights and disabled people*, Liberty, London.

Martin, J. and White, A. (1988) *The Financial Circumstances of Disabled Adults Living in Private Households*, OPCS, London.

Middleton, L. (1997) *The Art of Assessment*, Venture Press, Birmingham.

Morris, J. (1991) *Community Care or Independent Living?* Joseph Rowntree Foundation, York.

Morris, J. (1993) *Pride Against Prejudice: Transforming Attitudes to Disability,* The Women's Press, London.

Oliver, M. (1991) Disability and Participation in the Labour Market. In Brown, P. and Scase, R. (eds) *Poor Work*, Open University Press, Milton Keynes.

Oliver, M. (1993) Disability and dependency: a creation of industrial societies? In Swain, J., Finkelstein, V., French, S., and Oliver, M. (eds) *Disabling Barriers – Enabling Environments*, Sage, London.

Oliver, M. (1996) *Understanding Disability: From theory to practice*, Macmillan, Basingstoke.

Oliver, M. and Barnes, C. (1993) Discrimination, disability and welfare: from needs to rights. In Swain, J., Finkelstein, V., French, S., and Oliver, M. (eds) *Disabling Barriers – Enabling Environments*, Sage, London.

Rights for Disabled People Now (1995) *Civil Rights or a Discriminating Law, Rights Now,* London.

Roush, S.E. (1986) Health professionals as contributors to attitudes towards persons with disabilities, *Physical Therapy*, 66, 10, 1551-4.

Saraga, E. (1993) The abuse of children. In Dallos, R. and Mclaughlin, E. (eds) *Social Problems and the Family*, Sage/Open University, London.

Shakespeare, T., Gillespie-Sells, K., and Davies, D. (1996) *The Sexual Politics of Disability: Untold Desires*, Cassell, London.

Skills for People (1994) *Looking Back, Looking Forward: 10 Years of Skills for People*, Skills for People, Newcastle.

Skills for People (1997) *Annual Report 1995 -1996*, Skills for People, Newcastle.

Sperlinger, A. (1997) Introduction. In O'Hara, J. and Sperlinger, A. (eds) *Adults with Learning Difficulties: a practical approach for health professionals*, John Wiley and Sons, Chichester.

Stevens, A. (1991) *Disability Issues: developing anti-discriminatory practice*, Central Council for Education and Training in Social Work, London.

Swain, J. (1993) *Working Together for Citizenship*, P555U Update Workbook, Open University, Milton Keynes

Swain, J. (1995) *The Use of Counselling Skills: A Guide for therapists*, Butterworth-Heinemann, Oxford.

Swain, J. and French, S. (1997) Whose tragedy?, *Therapy Weekly*, 24,13, 7.

Swain, J. and French, S. (1998) Measuring up to normality: The foundations of disabling care. In Brechin, A., Katz, J., Walmsley, J. and Peace, S. (eds) *Care Matters: concepts, practice and research*, Sage, London.

References

Swain, J. and Lawrence, P. (1994) Learning about disability: changing attitudes or challenging understanding? In French, S. (ed) *On Equal Terms: Working with disabled people*, Butterworth-Heinemann, Oxford.

Thompson, N. (1997) *Anti-Discriminatory Practice*, Second Edition, Macmillan, London.

Trade Union Disability Alliance (1997) *Why the Disability Discrimination Act must be Repealed and Replaced with Civil Rights for Disabled People*, Trade Union Disability Alliance, Warwick.

Vass, A. A. (ed) (1996) *Social work competencies: core knowledge value and skills*. Sage Publications, London.

Wendell, S. (1996) *The Rejected Body: Feminist philosophical reflections on disability*, Routledge, London.

Wright, L. (1995) Take it from us: Training by people who know what they are talking about. In Philpot, T. and Ward, L. (eds) *Values and Visions: Changing Ideas in Services for People with Learning Difficulties*, Butterworth-Heinemann, Oxford.